Dedicated to all the people who carry on the *hoe wa'a* tradition, especially my dad, a canoe paddler since 1976.

First Edition 2008
ISBN: 978-0-615-18942-0
US $16.95
Library of Congress Control Number: 2008900904
Printed in Singapore by Star Standard Industries (Pte)Ltd.
Art Scanned by Maui Giclee
Printed on recyled paper

Text & Illustrations © by Maile Getzen 2008. All rights reserved. No part of this book may be reproduced in whole or in part in any form or by any means without prior written permission. Inquiries should be directed to maile@getzengalleries.com

Hawaiian proverb printed with permission from Bishop Museum Press, 'Ōlelo No'eau, 1983

P.O. Box 214, Hāna, Maui, 96713

Gift From the Forest

Written & Illustrated by Maile Getzen

I ulu no ka lālā i ke kumu

The branches grow because of the trunk.

Without our ancestors we would not be here.

ʻŌlelo Noʻeau

Long ago on the island of Maui,
a *koa* seedling pushed through the volcanic soil.

'Amakihi, 'elepaio, and 'i'iwi birds announced the birth from branch to branch.

A chorus of wind and leaves whispered, "Grow and sing with us."

Grow it did! Each year the tree's roots clung deeper and its branches reached higher than other trees.

But it didn't look very tall because its trunk leaned towards the sea.

One day a boy named Keola and his grandpa hiked with others up the steep slopes of Haleakalā. They searched for a tree to build a *kialoa*, a racing canoe, and it had to be a *koa* tree like the Hawaiians have used for thousands of years. It would honor their ancestors. And with a *koa* canoe they could race in the State Regatta.

Grandpa, who everyone called Papa, was a great canoe builder, a *kahuna kalai wa'a* from Tahiti. Papa touched one *koa* tree and said, "This tree is too small." He walked to another *koa* tree. "See how the *'elepaio* pecks this one? The wood will be full of bugs."

It was hard to find a tree, since *koa* had been cut down for its exquisite wood, and the habitat had been destroyed by invasive species like goats, cattle, and exotic plants.

While Papa and the others continued to search, Keola wandered off to pick *'ōhelo* berries. He was used to playing on his own while the adults worked. He hiked down into a little valley. Right when he popped a handful of red berries into his mouth, his brown eyes met the yellow eyes of a *pueo*, an owl. He reached out to touch her, but she swooped up to the high branches of a *koa* tree.

Keola turned his baseball hat around. Now he could see the top of the tree.

"Papa!" he called. His grandpa was too far away to hear. "Papa!" he yelled again. The sun was going over the mountain.

At last, he heard someone call, "Keola!"

"Over here!" Keola replied. He waited by the tree that leaned towards the sea until Papa found him. Papa touched the rough bark and said to the tree, "I can see the canoe in you."

Excitement hummed through the forest. In a ceremony Keola watched his aunty bury an offering of salt and fish by the tree. He looked in his backpack to see if he had anything to give, but he only had empty candy wrappers.

Keola was exhausted from hiking all day. He fell asleep as soon as his uncle started to play his 'ukulele.

At dawn Papa started the chain saw. It was all that could be heard until, creak, creak, CRACK, Boom!

The tree landed on a bed of *hāpuʻu* ferns. Keola felt the earth shake under his feet. He ran his hand over the stump of the tree and counted 137 rings. A wave of sadness swept over him and he whispered, "Don't be afraid *koa* tree, you will race over the ocean for a hundred more years."

Papa roughed out the shape of the canoe. He left a knob at the bow, the front, and a knob at the stern, the back, to haul the unfinished canoe, called the *kaʻele*, out of the forest.

Several people suggested using a helicopter to lift the log out of the forest. Papa said, "No, this part we must do as our ancestors did. We must take this log down the mountain, and our strength, our *mana*, will live forever in this wood."

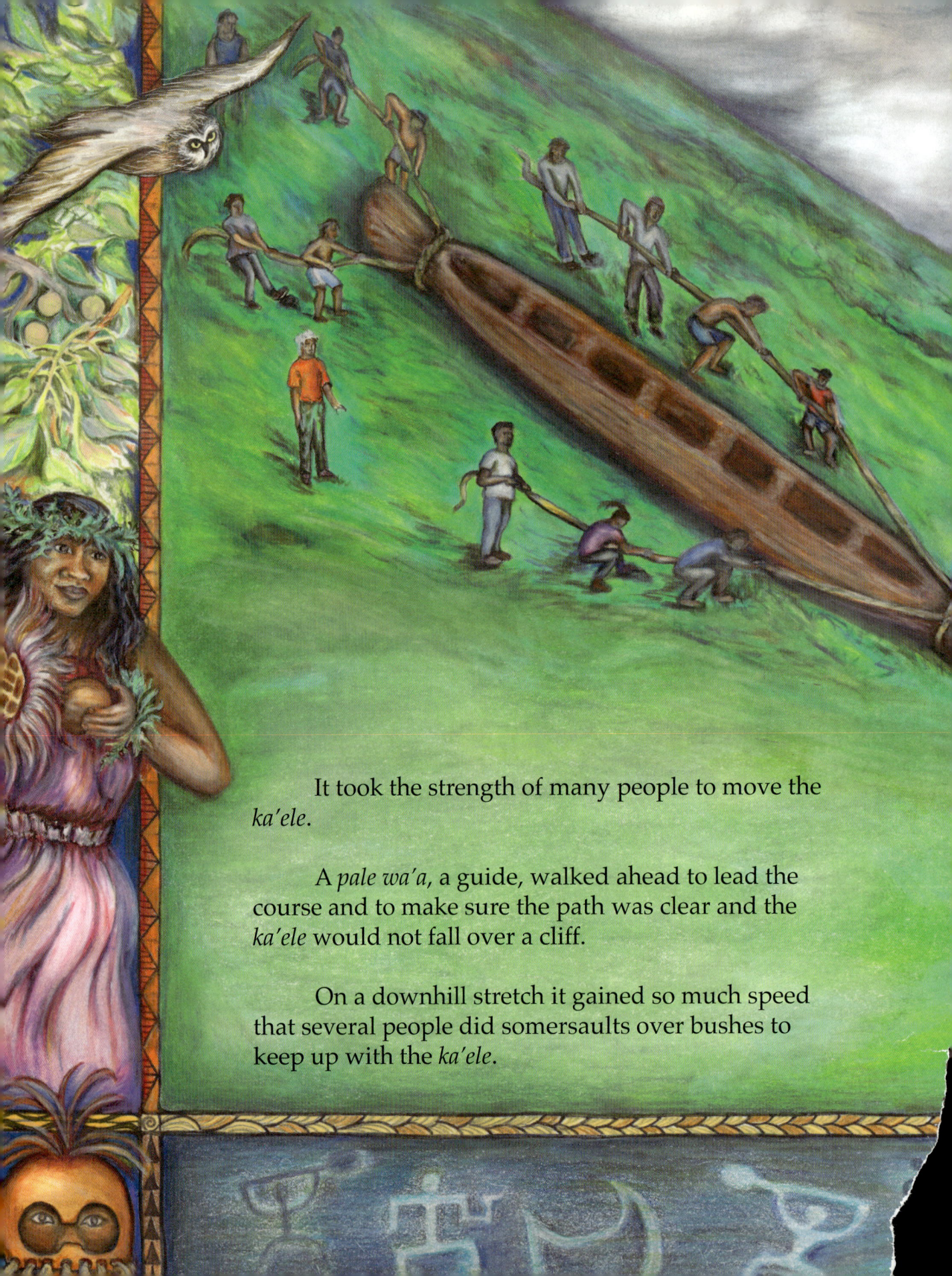

It took the strength of many people to move the *kaʻele*.

A *pale waʻa*, a guide, walked ahead to lead the course and to make sure the path was clear and the *kaʻele* would not fall over a cliff.

On a downhill stretch it gained so much speed that several people did somersaults over bushes to keep up with the *kaʻele*.

On the uphill stretch everyone chanted, *"Huki, Huki!"* Pull, Pull!

Keola slipped in the mud and fell more than once, but he did not let go. He held on tight to the rope, past deep ravines, over rocks and streams.

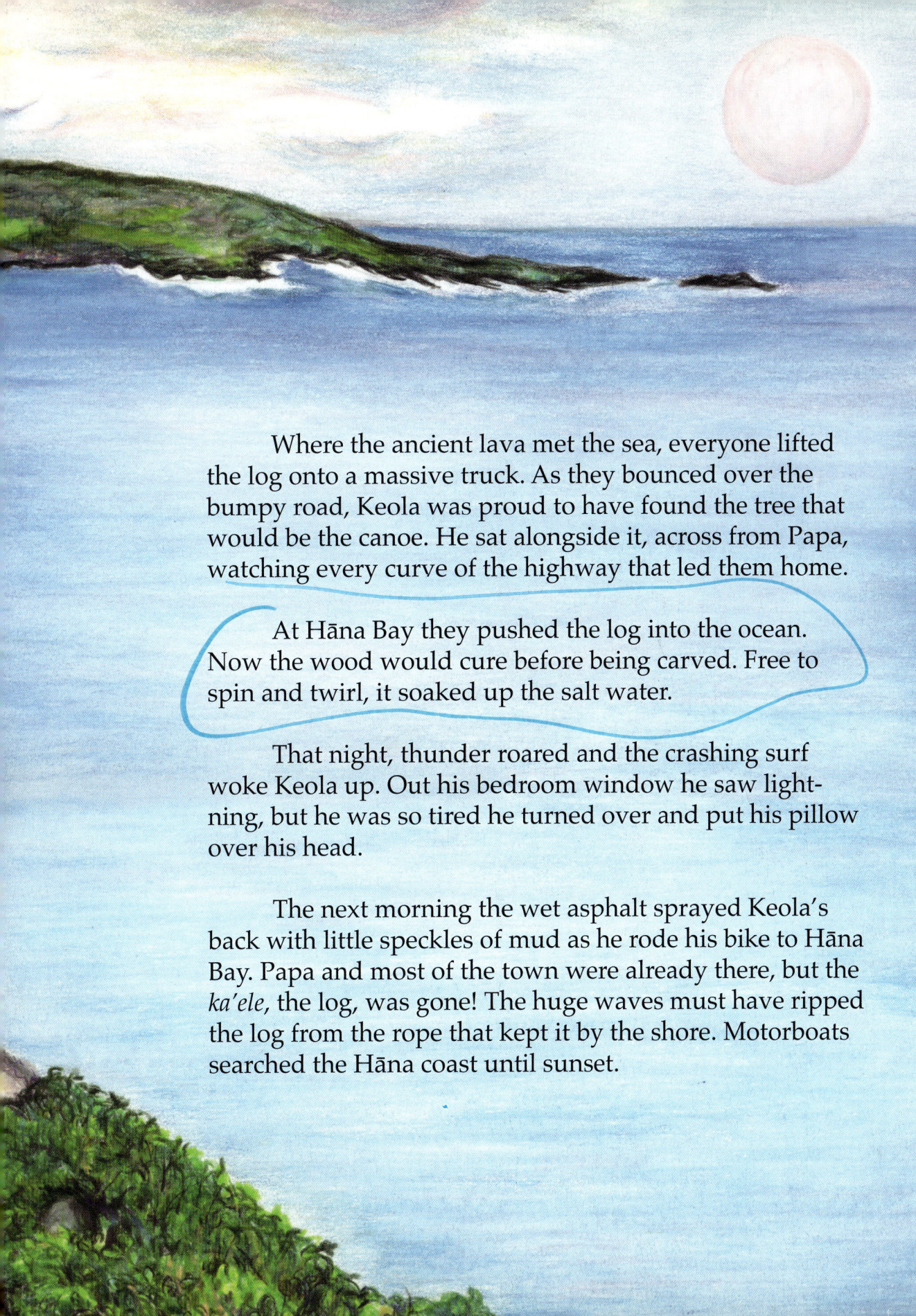

Where the ancient lava met the sea, everyone lifted the log onto a massive truck. As they bounced over the bumpy road, Keola was proud to have found the tree that would be the canoe. He sat alongside it, across from Papa, watching every curve of the highway that led them home.

At Hāna Bay they pushed the log into the ocean. Now the wood would cure before being carved. Free to spin and twirl, it soaked up the salt water.

That night, thunder roared and the crashing surf woke Keola up. Out his bedroom window he saw lightning, but he was so tired he turned over and put his pillow over his head.

The next morning the wet asphalt sprayed Keola's back with little speckles of mud as he rode his bike to Hāna Bay. Papa and most of the town were already there, but the *ka'ele*, the log, was gone! The huge waves must have ripped the log from the rope that kept it by the shore. Motorboats searched the Hāna coast until sunset.

The next day there was still no *ka'ele*, no log to make a canoe for the community, and no canoe to race in the State Regatta. Papa said, "The last *koa* canoe built in Hāna was seventy years ago. We may not find another tree while I am still alive."

Keola wasn't the most skilled diver, but he knew he had to find the log. He grabbed his mask and diving spear and jumped off the wharf. Swimming under the rusty concrete gave him the creeps, but he searched until he was sure it wasn't there.

He swam towards the lighthouse. As he got closer to the rocky cove a wave crashed over him and he lost his spear. Keola dove down to the bottom of the sea. He found his spear and pulled on it with all his might, but it stuck. He was running out of breath. It felt like his chest was going to burst. Keola shot out of the water gasping for air.

Just as he caught his breath, he saw a huge shadow move at the bottom of the ocean.

His spear bobbed out of the water. Keola's heart raced with fear. He lifted himself up on a rock and scraped his knee. "Ow!" he cried.

His knee stung and started to bleed. A *honu*, a turtle, peeked his head up and ducked back into the water. The shadow moved faster to the surface of the water.

Keola shrieked then yelled out, "It's the *ka'ele*, the log!"

Fishermen on the wharf jumped in the water to help bring it to shore. They congratulated Keola and told him it must be time to learn about shaping the canoe.

At the *hale wa'a*, the canoe house, Keola watched Papa transform the rough wood into a smooth canoe.

Papa told Keola to feel the little ledge at the stern, the back part of the canoe. "This seat, the *moamoa* is a seat for our ancestors. When the Hawaiians left Raiatea, Tahiti, a priest begged to go along, but they said, 'It's too full. There is no room for you!' However, the priest saw this little ledge, hopped on, and went all the way to Hawai'i with them. Now every canoe in Hawai'i has one, even the fiberglass canoes."

Keola ran his fingers over the one-inch seat. He tried to imagine a very small priest sitting there from Tahiti to Hawai'i.

Days turned into weeks. Keola's excitement of working on the canoe began to fade. He wished he could go play video games, or baseball, or anything besides sweeping sawdust and sanding. Finally, Papa said, "One more time over here and we can apply the finish." Keola's heart surged with joy when the dry pale wood turned a glossy red brown.

At sunrise a woman's chanting summoned everyone to celebrate the dawning of the tree's life as a *wa'a*, a canoe.

Kahuna Tau'a asked people to join in an *'awa* ceremony to honor the canoe. When the *'awa* bowl was passed around only the person with the bowl could talk.

The bowl came to Keola. He took a sip and said,

"Hāna Bay's Hawaiian name is Kapueokahi, the lone owl. In the forest an owl, a *pueo*, led us to this tree. Now this canoe will glide over the water like the *pueo* flies through the forest."

He passed the bowl to his grandpa on his left. He felt just like one of the men.

Papa took a drink and said, "Even if I was the strongest person in the world I couldn't make this canoe by myself. *Mahalo*, thank you, to everyone who keeps the *waʻa* tradition alive."

　While dancers chanted onshore, everyone carried the canoe into the ocean.

　Keola was told to jump into the front seat. Papa sat in the last seat calling out *"Hoʻomākaukau"* Prepare yourself, *"Hoe hapai!"* Lift your paddles! *"Huki!"* Pull! In unison the crew plunged in their paddles and pulled. Faster and faster the canoe slipped through the water. Keola's chest swelled with pride; he knew they could race in the State Regatta with their own canoe.

The crew paddled hard to catch a wave. Suddenly they were zooming fast. Keola lifted his paddle and screamed with excitement.

The *ama*, the outrigger, lifted out of the water and it felt like the canoe might flip over. The crew yelled, "Lean towards the *ama*!"

White bubbles of foam crashed over them. Keola wanted to surf another wave, but more people were waiting to ride the canoe.

Onshore Keola and Papa watched people paddle around the bay. Papa said, "This is the fastest canoe I have ever built."

"Me, too," Keola replied. Papa laughed.

"Don't laugh, Papa!" Keola said, "For real, when my kids paddle in this canoe it will still be the fastest."

Papa whispered, "Tell them to cup their ears next to the *kino*, the body of the canoe. Maybe they'll hear the soft rustle of *koa* leaves."

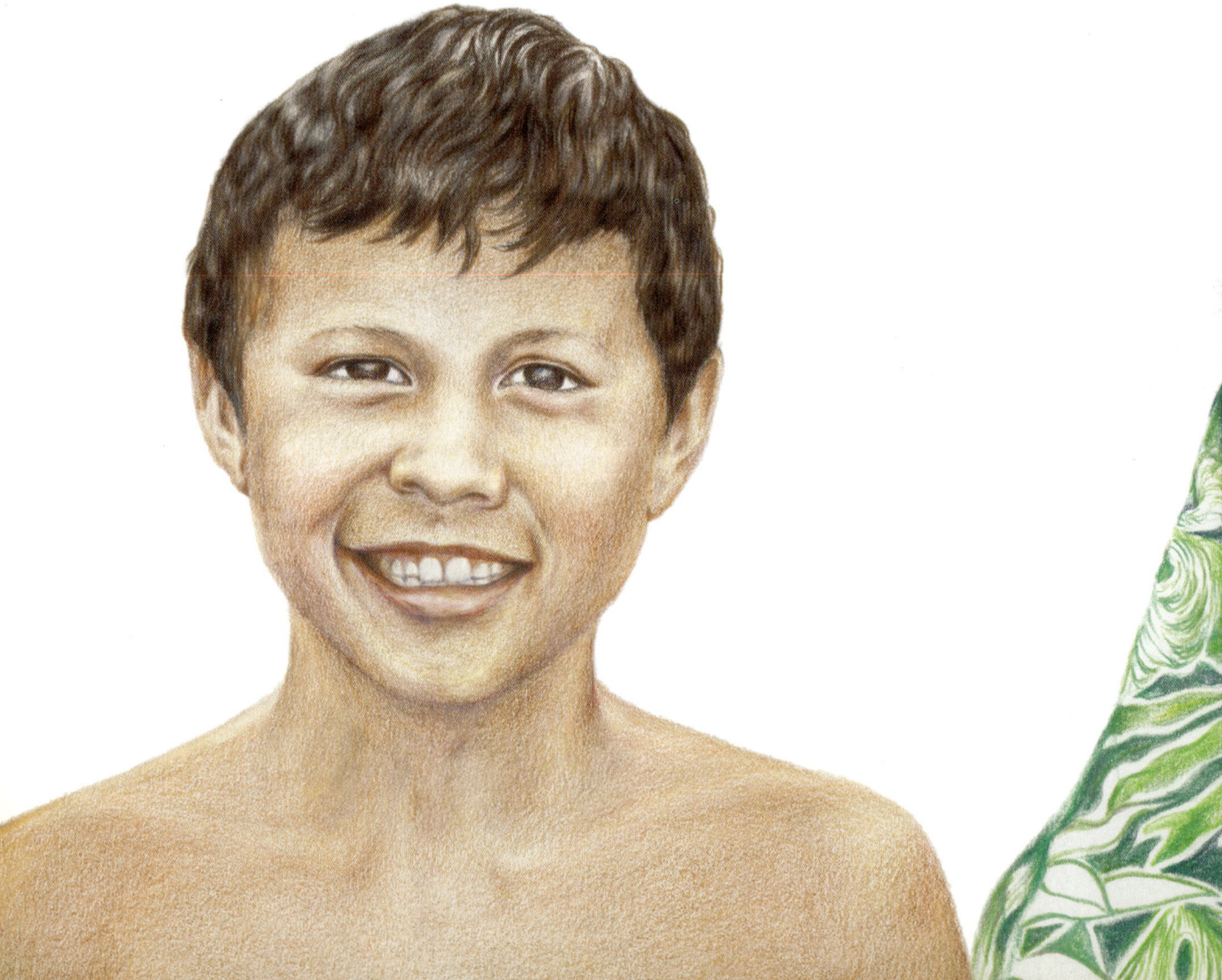

Canoe Racing

The canoe, the *wa'a*, is more than a boat. It is a vessel that unites the Polynesian people. In New Zealand/Aotearoa, Tahiti, Tonga, Samoa, Fiji, Marquesas, Cook Islands, and Hawai'i, the canoe was used for transport, for fishing, for war, and for sport.

Canoe racing requires an enormous amount of stamina, split-second timing, and teamwork. Six men or women make a team: The first seat sets the pace. The second usually calls the changes—fourteen on the left, fourteen on the right. Three and five paddle with the first man, four and six with number two. The sixth man is also the steersman.

In Hawai'i, there are canoe clubs on every island. Ages ranging from nine to over seventy make paddling a family sport. The regatta season begins in May and ends in August with the state races, where every canoe must be of traditional *koa*. The distance season continues through the fall, culminating with Nā Wāhine O Ke Kai and The Moloka'i Hoe, a race across the Kaiwi Channel from Moloka'i to O'ahu. To race in a *koa* canoe is to become part of a 3,000-year-old heritage. Youngsters learn about *'ohana*, family, *lōkahi*, working together, and they experience the exhilaration and celebration at the end of the race.

A True Story

In the Hawaiian Islands, few *kahuna kālai waʻa*, master canoe carvers, are alive to perpetuate the cultural tradition of building a *koa* canoe. In the 1900s new roads and steamships in Hawaiʻi led to an end of the canoe as a way of life. The *koa* itself has been overharvested and exported for its exquisite wood. Goats, cattle, and invasive species have demolished much of the native forests. Today conservation efforts to replant and fence off areas are ensuring the *koa's* survival for future generations.

In 2000, a *kālai waʻa* from Tahiti, Fafa Toofa, brought his knowledge to Hāna, Maui. The seed for this book grew as I watched Fafa, his son-in-law, Alexi, his grandson Leon, and my dad, Bob Getzen, put the finishing touches on a *kialoa*, a *koa* outrigger racing canoe.

People from all over Maui helped build the canoe. They learned the process and protocol of taking a tree from the mountains, and the traditions, blessings, and chants involved in the transformation of the tree to a canoe in the sea. To build a canoe takes many hands. They all became a part of giving the canoe life.

The canoe was named Te Tāne Hāna Hoe, and raced in the State Regatta.

In Hāna, Maui on June 25, 2005, Leon Teamo "Fafa" Toofa passed away.

When Fafa was nine years old he lost his father. In Pueu, Tahiti, he spent his days watching his grandfather carve canoes. At that time, the chain saw didn't exist, so using an adz made of sharpened rock, a wooden handle, and some rope he built his first canoe. Over the years he became an expert with the chain saw. He built over 300 racing canoes in wood and fiberglass. He also coached the championship canoe club Taiarapu Nui. On Maui he helped the Kīhei, Hāna, and Hawaiian canoe clubs fulfill their dreams of building a traditional *koa* canoe.

In 2003, I showed Fafa the illustrations for this book. When I gave him a copy of his portrait, he touched the eyes, the nose, and then the mouth of the drawing. He said, "I like this picture. Now I have new teeth, so you can do one more and I'll smile real big." He flashed a wide grin and had his characteristic *kolohe*, playful, sparkle in his eyes.

Resources:
At www.getzengalleries.com and at www.mauicanoefest.com, there are more photos, and links about the the *wa'a*. At www.jazzalleytv.com, you will find, "Wa'a Ho'olaule'a (Festival of Canoes)", a film by Kenneth K. Martinez Burgmaier. The following books have detailed information about canoe building, traditions, and racing:

Caldwell, Peter. Molokai-Oahu *Through the Years: A History of the Molokai Outrigger Canoe Race*. HI, Editions Limited, 2006.

Chun, Naomi N. Y. *Hawaiian Canoe Building Traditions*. Rev. ed. Illustrated by Robin Y. Burningham. Honolulu, HI.: Kamehameha Schools/Bernice Pauahi Bishop Estate, 1995.

Holmes, Tommy. *The Hawaiian Canoe*. HI: Editions Limited, 1981.

About the Author

Maile Getzen was born and raised in Hāna, Maui. After attending college in México, teaching Art and Spanish in Seattle and earning her Masters in Education, she returned home to Hawai'i where she continues to teach, paint and write.

"Keola", Rodney Akau, paddles for Hawaiian Canoe Club.

Photographers:
Carol Friedman, Pam Carroll, Maile Atay, Buddy Greig, Maile Getzen.

People in Photos pages 30-33: Leon Temanupaioura, Shaunie Naauao-Keanini, Mahea Naeole, Ivy Kaanana, Thomas "Ko'i" Lum, Alika Atay, Ano Mederois, Paul Luuwai, Leland Camara, Jerry Pahukoa, Bob Getzen, Alexi Reid-Haiti, Charlie Noland, Zaida Bradley, Bill Monahan, Bully Ho'opai, Moses Timbal, Bruce Stoner, Peter Sinenci, Rick Rutiz, Barry Chang, Don Atay, Mike Woessner, Tim Everett, Paul Bodnar, Hatota Tehiva, Skippy Young, Bally Helekahi, Robert and Pat Malaiakini, Edward Olivera, Pam Carroll, Perry Bednorz, Pakalana Helekahi, Tiny Kapoe, Leimamo Naihe.

Models in llustrations: Rodney Akau, Keli'i Tau'a, Bob Getzen, Lovie Bednorz, Nalani Kuailani, and Fafa Toofa. Hana Girls Crew: Mino Kapoe, Sherae Hanchett, Kilani Krause, Kalena Aina, Chelsea Emmsley, and Sadie Ferris.

Mahalo Nui Loa

Like building a canoe, a book takes many hands to create. *Gift from the Forest*, was made possible with the help and inspiration of Maria Inigues; Bob Getzen; Sydney Jamison-Sakugawa; David Sakugawa; Liz Barber; Kirsten Whatley; Buddy Greig; Lori Gomez; Josephine Blair; Carol Friedman; Charlie Noland; Kyle Tate; Gerald McDermott; Tammy Yee; Judi Riley; Barb Powers; Holly Cupala; David Edgerton; Ken Kennell; Molly Murrah; Alyssa Mendez de Leon, Gwyneth Kozma; Robin and Sydney White; Mary Anne Wormsted; Tom Barber; Gena Sansone; Linda Gravatt; Richard and Susie Watson; the Akaus: Shani, Rodney, Taylor, Linnie, Tessa, and Elaina; Rob Ratkowski; Pekelo Cosma; Dave Takaki; Kenny Martinez-Burgmaier; Mike Tavioni; Fafa Toofa and his Ohana.

A special thank-you to everyone who participated in the making of the koa canoe, and to all the people that hosted and helped Fafa in Maui: "Bully" Kimokeo Kapahulehua, Bob Bradley, Charlie and Ben Noland, Paul Luuwai, Coila Eade, Francis Sinenci, Earl and Naomi Kuailani, Robert and Pat Malaiakini, The Redo's, Mike Woessner, Hanky "Boy" Eharris, Colleen Ford, Ray Hutaff, Tim Everett, Maile and Alika Atay, Don and Daniela Atay, Mael and Magdalena Carey, Kalani English, Karen Davidson, Hatota Tehiva, and many others.